FLYING FIDDLE DUETS

for two cellos

book one   Myanna Harvey

CHP272

Cover painting by Gregory El Harvey
For more information, visit www.gregharveygallery.com

Flying Fiddle Duets for Two Cellos

Traditional Tunes, arranged by Myanna Harvey

Tableof Contents

Flying Fiddle Duets for Two Cellos, Book One

John Ryan's Polka

Trad., arr. Myanna Harvey

The Irish Washerwoman

Trad., arr. M. Harvey

6

Swallowtail Jig

Trad., arr. M. Harvey

Johnny's Gone for a Soldier

Trad., arr. M. Harvey

8

Drunken Sailor

Trad., arr. M. Harvey

Greensleeves

Trad., arr. M. Harvey

Soldier's Joy

Trad., arr. M. Harvey

14

Star of the County Down

Trad., arr. M. Harvey

The Water is Wide

Trad., arr. M. Harvey

Lannigan's Ball

Trad., arr. M. Harvey

1812 Quickstep

Trad., arr. M. Harvey

20

Shenandoah

Trad., arr. M. Harvey

All the Pretty Horses

Trad., arr. M. Harvey

This Page Left Blank
to Eliminate Page Turns

Fire in the Mountain

Trad., arr. M. Harvey

Devil Among the Tailors

Trad., arr. M. Harvey

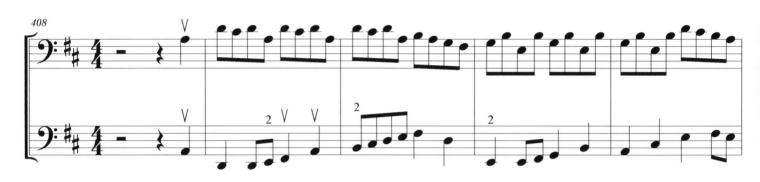

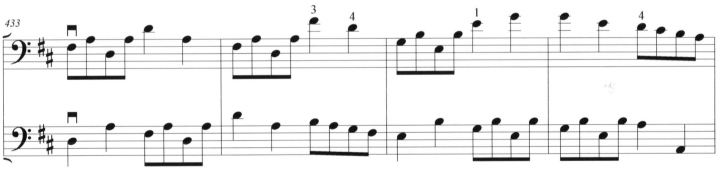

28

Liberty

Trad., arr. M. Harvey

The Girl I Left Behind Me

Trad., arr. M. Harvey

Ballad of the Green Mountain Boys

Trad., arr. M. Harvey

St. Patrick's Day

Trad., arr. M. Harvey

The Triplet Book for Cello, Part One

1

Left-Hand Warm-Up

Cassia Harvey

60248798R00023

Made in the USA
Lexington, KY
01 February 2017